June/Junio

By/Por Robyn Brode

Reading Consultant/Consultora de lectura: Linda Cornwell,
Literacy Connections Consulting/consultora de lectoescritura

WEEKLY READER®

PUBLISHING

Please visit our web site at **www.garethstevens.com**.
For a free catalog describing our list of high-quality books, call 1-800-542-2595 (USA)
or 1-800-387-3178 (Canada). Our fax: 1-877-542-2596

Library of Congress Cataloging-in-Publication Data
Brode, Robyn.
    [Junio. Spanish & English]
    June / by Robyn Brode ; reading consultant, Linda Cornwell — Junio / por Robyn Brode ;
    consultora de lectura, Linda Cornwell.
       p. cm. — (Months of the year — Meses del año)
    English and Spanish in parallel text.
    Includes bibliographical references and index.
    ISBN-10: 1-4339-1934-6   ISBN-13: 978-1-4339-1934-3 (lib. bdg.)
    ISBN-10: 1-4339-2111-1   ISBN-13: 978-1-4339-2111-7 (softcover)
    1. June (Month)—Juvenile literature. 2. Holidays—United States—Juvenile literature.
  3. Vacations—United States—Juvenile literature. I. Cornwell, Linda. II. Title. III. Title: Junio.
  GT4803.B768   2010b
  394.263—dc22   2009013982

This edition first published in 2010 by
Weekly Reader® Books
An Imprint of Gareth Stevens Publishing
1 Reader's Digest Road
Pleasantville, NY 10570-7000 USA

Executive Managing Editor: Lisa M. Herrington
Senior Editors: Barbara Bakowski, Jennifer Magid-Schiller
Designer: Jennifer Ryder-Talbot
Translators: Tatiana Acosta and Guillermo Gutiérrez

Photo Credits: Cover, back cover, title © SW Productions/Getty Images; p. 7 © Masterfile; p. 9
© Bobbi Lane/Weekly Reader; pp. 11, 17, 19, 21 © Ariel Skelley/Weekly Reader; p. 13 © Blend
Images Photography/Veer; p. 15 © Ryan McVay/Getty Images

Printed in the United States of America

1 2 3 4 5 6 7 8 9 10 11 10 09

Table of Contents/Contenido

Boldface words appear in the glossary.

Las palabras en **negrita** aparecen en el glosario.

Welcome to June!

June is the sixth month of the year.

June has 30 days.

— — — — — — — — —

¡Bienvenidos a junio!

Junio es el sexto mes del año.

Junio tiene 30 días.

Months of the Year/Meses del año

Month/Mes	Number of Days/ Días en el mes
1 January/Enero	31
2 February/Febrero	28 or 29*/28 ó 29*
3 March/Marzo	31
4 April/Abril	30
5 May/Mayo	31
6 June/Junio	**30**
7 July/Julio	31
8 August/Agosto	31
9 September/Septiembre	30
10 October/Octubre	31
11 November/Noviembre	30
12 December/Diciembre	31

*February has an extra day every fourth year./Febrero tiene un día extra cada cuatro años. **5**

In June, spring ends and **summer** begins. Summer begins on June 20 or 21.

– – – – – – – – – –

En junio, se acaba la primavera y empieza el **verano**. El verano comienza el 20 ó 21 de junio.

The first day of summer is the longest day of the year. It has more hours of sunlight than any other day.

— — — — — — — — —

El primer día del verano es el más largo del año. Es el día que tiene más horas de luz.

In many places, June is warm and sunny. Sunshine helps plants and flowers grow.

— — — — — — — — —

En muchos lugares, en junio hace un tiempo agradable y soleado. La luz solar ayuda a que las flores y las plantas crezcan.

What kinds of flowers grow where you live?

— — — — — — —

¿Qué tipo de flores crecen en el lugar donde vives?

flowers/
flores

11

Special Days

June 14 is **Flag Day**. On that day, Americans honor our country's flag.

— — — — — — — — —

Días especiales

El 14 de junio es el **Día de la Bandera**. Ese día, los estadounidenses honramos la bandera de nuestro país.

The third Sunday in June is Father's Day. Kids give cards and gifts to dads and other men who are important to them.

— — — — — — — — — —

El tercer domingo de junio es el Día del Padre. Los niños entregan tarjetas y regalos a su papá y a otros hombres importantes en su vida.

School Is Out!

In some places, school ends in June. Summer **vacation** begins.

— — — — — — — — —

¡Se acabaron las clases!

En algunos lugares, el año escolar termina en junio. Empiezan las **vacaciones** de verano.

 How will you spend your summer vacation?

— — — — — — —

¿Qué vas a hacer en tus vacaciones de verano?

Many friends have fun at the playground in summer.

— — — — — — — — —

En el verano, muchos amigos se divierten en el parque.

**playground/
parque**

When June ends, it is time for July
to begin.

— — — — — — — — — —

Cuando junio termina, empieza julio.

Glossary/Glosario

Flag Day: a day to honor the American flag, celebrated on June 14

summer: the season between spring and fall, when the weather is the warmest of the year

vacation: time away from school or work

▬ ▬ ▬ ▬ ▬ ▬ ▬ ▬ ▬

Día de la Bandera: 14 de junio, día en que se honra la bandera de Estados Unidos

vacaciones: periodo de descanso de las actividades de la escuela o del trabajo

verano: la estación del año entre la primavera y el otoño. Es la época más calurosa del año.

For More Information/Más información

Books/Libros

Flag Day/Día de la Bandera. Our Country's Holidays/Las fiestas de nuestra nación (series). Sheri Dean (Gareth Stevens Publishing, 2006)

Summer/Verano. Seasons of the Year/Las estaciones del año (series). JoAnn Early Macken (Gareth Stevens Publishing, 2006)

Web Sites/Páginas web

Father's Day Games and Activities/Actividades y juegos del Día del Padre
www.apples4theteacher.com/holidays/fathers-day
Find poems about dads, games, and coloring pages./Encuentren poemas sobre los padres, así como juegos y páginas para colorear.

Flag Day/Día de la Bandera
www.enchantedlearning.com/crafts/flagday
Make red, white, and blue crafts./Hagan manualidades rojas, blancas y azules.

Index/Índice

About the Author

Robyn Brode has been a teacher, a writer, and an editor in the book publishing field for many years. She earned a bachelor's degree in English literature from the University of California, Berkeley.

Información sobre la autora

Robyn Brode ha sido maestra, escritora y editora de libros durante muchos años. Obtuvo su licenciatura en literatura inglesa en la Universidad de California, Berkeley.